# LIFE BEGINS

## Quran Stories for Little Hearts

by

## S Khan

Goodword**kidz**

*Helping you build a family of faith*

Long long ago, there was no earth,
No sky, no sun or moon.
There was darkness everywhere.
Then Allah thought of making
a beautiful world —
A world full of purpose.
Allah just said the words
And there was the earth and the sky.
There was the bright sun,
The shining moon and
twinkling stars.

3

Then came the dry land and the oceans.
By just saying the words, Allah made them all.
Allah made the earth in two days.
On it He placed very big mountains.

In two days He formed the sky into seven heavens.
The lowest heaven He hung with brilliant stars
And sent bright comets,
Flying between them.

Allah made the earth
Circle around the sun
So that there would be
Night and day and
Many different seasons too.

9

Allah filled
The vast universe
With thousands of stars
And many planets
All spinning swiftly,
But never touching each other.

Allah made lovely flowers —
Roses and pansies,
Bluebells and lupins,
Hollyhocks and daisies.
Where did the flowers come from?
Allah made them all.

He made all things large and tiny.
Little insects, and black ants
That crawl around on the ground.
And the busy bees
That fly from flower to flower
To collect sweet honey.

14

Allah made juicy fruits —
Mangoes, oranges and cherries,
Crunchy apples, sweet grapes
And soft bananas.
Where did the fruits come from?
Allah made them all.

Allah made the animals.
Some live in the forests.
Large elephants,
Fat hippos,
Cunning foxes,
Fierce tigers,
Striped zebras
And tall giraffes.
Fluffy rabbits,
Strong horses,
Grazing cows and sheep —
Allah made them all.

17

Beautiful birds flying in the sky —
Spreading their wings and closing them.
Green parrots, white ducks,
Colourful chickens, flying sparrows,
Dancing peacocks, singing quails,
Diving kingfishers, warbling larks,
And many, many more.
Where did they all come from?
Allah made them all.

Allah made the large oceans
And the big seas
Which cover the earth with water
And form into
Deep lakes and long rivers.
Allah made the sea monsters
And all the fishes
Big and small —
Large blue whales
Like mountains,
And cruel tiger sharks
With big jaws.

Allah made the crabs
And lobsters and shrimps,
Huge eels and octopuses,
Swordfish and jelly fish,
And all the many
Ocean plants and animals.

Allah gave us rain
And sunshine,
Cool breezes and clouds
Passing by.
Thank You, Allah,
For making
Such a wonderful world.